WE ARE THE
ROMANS

Meet the people behind the history

David Long

Illustrated by Allen Fatimaharan

WELBECK

Published in 2021 by Welbeck Children's Books

An imprint of Welbeck Children's Limited,
part of Welbeck Publishing Group.
20 Mortimer Street, London W1T 3JW

Text © David Long 2021
Illustrations © Allen Fatimaharan 2021

Managing Art Editor: Matt Drew
Associate Publisher: Laura Knowles
Editor: Jenni Lazell

ISBN 978-1-78312-605-7

Printed in Heshan, China

10 9 8 7 6 5 4 3 2 1

CONTENTS

WE ARE THE ROMANS

Salve! (That's Latin for "Hello!") You are about to set off on a tour of the Roman Empire, but this isn't a tour of dusty old ruined buildings or statues of pompous Emperors. No, instead you will meet real Romans. People who went to work or school, ate their dinner, and went to the bathroom. In lots of ways, Roman lives were just the same as yours, but in other ways, they were very different. We hope you enjoy getting to know us!

WHAT WAS THE ROMAN EMPIRE?

Nearly 2,000 years ago the Romans ruled the largest empire the world had ever seen. From their capital in what is now Italy, an army of highly trained and well-armed soldiers had successfully conquered vast areas of Europe, Africa, and Asia. This included modern countries such as England and Wales, Spain, Portugal, France, Germany, Greece, and Turkey, as well as Egypt and several smaller ones in north Africa.

Many of the people the Romans defeated were captured and made slaves, but millions of others were eventually allowed to become Roman citizens or to join the army. They learned to speak Latin, the official language of the empire, and hundreds of new towns and cities were constructed for citizens to live in.

For centuries, the Roman army was at war and countless people were killed in battle. However, the Romans also played an important part in improving the lives of ordinary people in the lands they conquered. So on the one hand, Rome was a brutal conqueror, but on the other hand, it shaped western civilization in many positive ways.

WHAT HAPPENED TO ROME?

Some historians think that the Roman Empire just became too successful to survive. By the fourth century it was too big for anyone to govern it effectively. At one point there were no fewer than four emperors all ruling at the same time, and it took weeks or even months for a person to travel from Rome to any of the farthest parts of the empire. After splitting into two (with two different capital cities) the empire gradually fell apart as neighboring tribes successfully attacked it from outside.

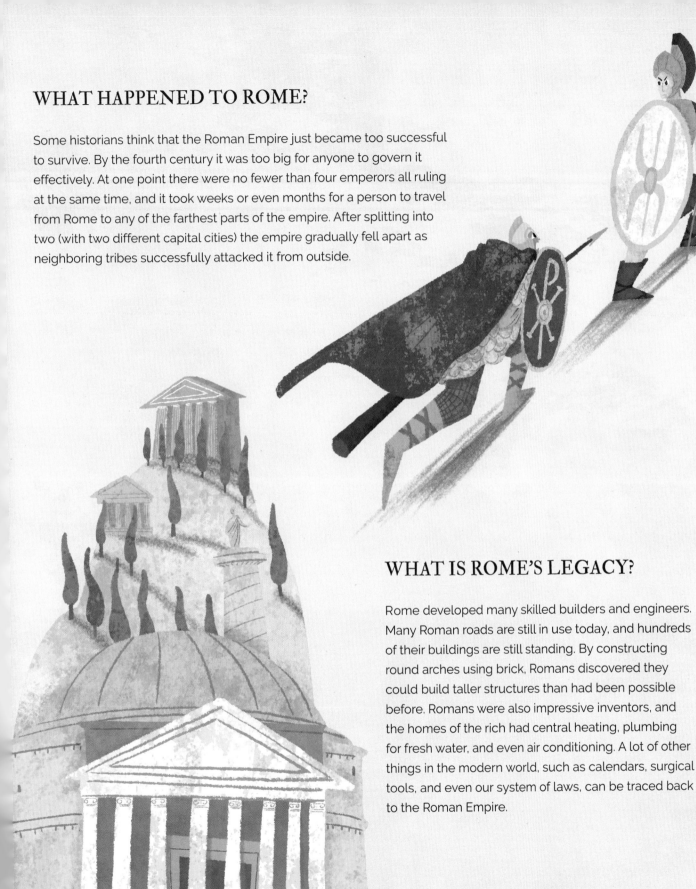

WHAT IS ROME'S LEGACY?

Rome developed many skilled builders and engineers. Many Roman roads are still in use today, and hundreds of their buildings are still standing. By constructing round arches using brick, Romans discovered they could build taller structures than had been possible before. Romans were also impressive inventors, and the homes of the rich had central heating, plumbing for fresh water, and even air conditioning. A lot of other things in the modern world, such as calendars, surgical tools, and even our system of laws, can be traced back to the Roman Empire.

I AM THE EMPEROR

My full name is Nerva Traianus Divi Nervae filius Augustus. It's difficult to say and even harder to remember, so my subjects know me best as Trajan or they just call me Caesar—the title that rulers of our mighty empire have used for a century or more.

I am an old man now and would like to spend more time in Rome. Traveling around such a huge empire is hard and takes time. I prefer my palaces. Most of my people have never seen me but they know my face because every Roman town and city has statues of me on its streets. There are also statues of those who were emperors before me.

As a young man, before I was emperor, I spent even more time abroad fighting battles against our enemies. I conquered new lands to make the empire even larger. Now it is the largest in the world and it would be impossible for a man to see it all in one lifetime. My advisers tell me it is more than two thousand miles from one end to the other.

Some emperors ruled because their fathers ruled before them, but I was chosen. Nerva, the previous emperor, chose me for my skill as a soldier. A man can have no greater honor, and in my turn I have chosen a cousin, Hadrian, to occupy the throne when I am gone.

Although I am old, no one is more powerful than I am. I have smart men to advise me. I have wise priests to guide me, and the greatest generals to fight my battles —but they all know that the emperor is in charge.

By controlling the Senate, where Roman laws are made, I control my empire. The army is mine. Its officers and men support me now, just as they supported the emperors of the past. They will support Hadrian and the other men who will come after my death.

With so much power, an emperor can be good or evil and Romans have lived under both. I admit I have ordered the deaths of many guilty men and women, but I have also let the innocent go free. In the same way, my army has killed thousands in battle, but they do this not for me but for the glory of Rome.

I AM A PATRICIAN

Everyone knows who I am because I am Titus Gallio Herma. I am an important man. I am a very rich man. I am a patrician.

For hundreds of years, Roman society was divided into patricians like me, and the ordinary people who we call plebians or just plebs. My father was a patrician, his father was a patrician before him, so was his father before that, and so on. That's always been how it works and it explains why I am a patrician.

Patricians were the rulers of Rome before I was born and the plebs were the people they ruled over. It's not like that now, but I wish it was! Now the Emperor rules all of us, although patricians like me are still important because we have money and power. I am much richer than any ordinary person, for example, and I have several large houses which are far more luxurious

than most ordinary ones. I have more slaves than I can even count, at least 400 of them, so I have never bothered learning any of their names. After all, they are only slaves.

Ordinary people don't seem to like me much, but I don't mind because I don't like them at all. One of my friends told me the plebs think I am rude and arrogant, but I don't know how they can think this because I never speak to them if I can help it. Naturally I much prefer spending my time with other important people and speaking to them instead. For example, I'm always telling politicians and army generals what I think they should do. Mind you, I have noticed that they don't always seem to be as interested in what I have to say as they used to be . . .

I AM A SLAVE BOY

My name is Bubo. I live in the home of my master,
Marcus Lucius, who tells me I am about ten years old.

Marcus Lucius is mostly kind, but I have to get up very early in the morning and I work hard every day. I sweep the house before anyone wakes up and I carry wood into the kitchen for the cook's fire. Later, I sweep the courtyard and sometimes I open the door to my master's guests. They are important people because my master is very rich.

If a slave has children, they all become slaves too, so my life has always been like this. My mother is dead now, but she was owned by my master. That means that he owns me too. Other slaves are bought and sold at slave markets, which I don't think I'd like.

I have to sleep on the floor, so I'm nearly always tired, but I've heard stories of many other slaves whose lives are much worse than mine. Some of them have cruel masters who bully them and beat them. Men, women, and even children work deep underground digging for tin and silver, or build houses beneath the burning sun. Anyone trying to escape is caught and punished, and a bad slave can be sold to somebody even worse!

My master has nine children and some of them look about the same age as me. In the summer I see them playing outside and laughing but I am never allowed to join in. None of the children ever speak to me or to any of the other slaves in the house unless they want to order us to do something for them.

Sweeping is boring, so when I am older I would like to be a cook. I spend as much time as I can in the kitchen, watching what the cook does so that one day I can do it too. He knows I want to do this and so he sometimes helps me by explaining what he is doing. I like the cook a lot, although he is very old.

I AM A FREED SLAVE

At least a quarter of the people in the Roman Empire work as slaves. I did too, once upon a time, but I am now a *liberta*, which is what we call a freed slave.

My name is Calista Sulla and I think I'm about 40, which is quite old for our people. I began working for my mistress when I was a little girl, but after 30 years she set me free. This is the Roman custom.

I am skilled—many slaves are—and for most of my life I stitched clothes by hand and made them just the way my mistress wanted them. I sewed the finest long tunics for her and her daughters, using rich, colored silks all the way from China, and the best Egyptian cotton.

I was proud of my work then, and many of my mistress's friends became jealous of her beautiful clothes and their high quality. Of course, like all slaves, I had to work long hours and often I pricked my hands with pins. This made them bleed and sting, but even so I still miss my old life sometimes.

Of course, I am very happy to be free and I still prick my fingers all the time. But, now that I work for the other people in the town, things are very different. They are nearly all poor like me, not rich like my old mistress. This means the work is still hard, but the clothes are never beautiful.

Ordinary people can't afford fine luxuries from China and Egypt, so I mostly work with sheep's wool now and sometimes a rough linen made from a plant called flax. My customers don't need beautiful clothes, just ones which last. Clothes that cover them up and keep them warm. No one comes to me for beautiful new tunics, just to stitch their old ones when these fall to pieces.

I AM A TEACHER

I am Ludus Andronicus and I teach boys from ages six to 12. We don't have school buildings like the ones you go to in modern times. Instead, the boys come to my house every day of the week and I have a special room here which I use for lessons.

I charge money for teaching, so the boys all come from the rich families of the town. Poor boys do not go to school, and neither do any girls, so only about a third of Romans ever learn to write.

Education begins at home for the privileged ones. Younger boys are taught to read and write in Latin. Mothers teach their girls how to run a home and how to be a good Roman wife. Families sometimes employ

a private tutor but when the boys come to me, it is to learn harder subjects such as mathematics and the Greek language. We educated Romans have always admired the Greeks for their learning and culture, so I base all my lessons on theirs. Writing is done on wax tablets with a sharp stylus because papyrus (a kind of paper made from reeds) is far too expensive to be wasted on children.

The students have to work hard when they come to me. Lessons often start before sunrise (I have plenty of oil lamps) and although the boys are allowed to nap after lunch, we start again afterwards and work until late afternoon. Hardly anyone misbehaves because I keep a cane by my side and the boys know I will beat them if they do.

When they turn twelve, most boys go straight to work but a few go to higher schools. There they study more Greek and Latin as well as literature and "oration," which is what we call learning to speak clearly and confidently to a room full of people. Many of the best orators eventually become politicians.

I AM A MUSICIAN

This is my *cithara,* and I am Titus Pansa the musician.

The Greeks say they are better performers than us, but we Romans love music too. One of our emperors used to play a cithara a bit like mine, another paid for pieces to be written for his favorite musicians. As for me, I make a living by playing my cithara for other people, usually at festivals and funerals, or to accompany a group of dancers.

The cithara is a bit like a harp, Some older Roman instruments were made from animal horns and tortoiseshell but this one is mostly of wood, which gives it such a rich, strong sound. And even with only seven strings, I can make so many different sounds. People listening to me play say that sometimes I make it sing but at other times it sounds just like crying. I'm very proud when I hear this because I always try to match the mood.

Rich Romans don't dance, but they like to pay dancers so they can watch—and dancers need music to dance to! I love playing in a group with other musicians who are my friends, and the music we make always sounds happy and lively.

These friends accompany me by blowing on a bronze tuba (which is longer than my legs) and a tibia which is formed by two pipes held side by side. They also have bells, rattles, and tambourines, and a type of rhythmic wooden foot clapper called a scabellum. Many children think this looks a bit like a Roman sandal but it helps us to play in time with each other.

No one in Rome ever grew rich by playing music, but mostly we don't mind because it's such a lovely thing to do.

I AM A MOSAIC MAKER

I'm Milonius the mosaic maker, and you'll see my work everywhere around our city.

Romans love mosaics and at my workshop we produce mosaic floors for private houses as well as for great public buildings. I tell my customers they're the only works of art they can walk on and mine are definitely works of art, although I admit I'm more of a craftsman than an artist who sculpts and paints.

Customers come to my workshop asking for all sorts of colorful designs and I'm happy to make whatever they want. I've made more than two hundred mosaics so far, showing every aspect of Roman life from family portraits to farming scenes, from weapons to wild animals. Recently I was even asked to show two gladiators fighting and I'm happy I finished that one last week.

Making even a small mosaic can take several days because it takes hundreds or even thousands of tiny cubes, or tesserae, to build a picture. Each cube is smaller than the nail on your little finger. They're mostly different colored rock or stone, although sometimes I use glass and even seashells to make a mosaic really come alive. It takes a lot of time to lay them out in the right pattern, especially when it is a large mosaic to fill a room. I also have to spend hours in the workshop before this, cutting these hard materials into shape.

Sometimes customers ask me what I like doing best. I tell them faces, because everyone has a face and I hope they're going to pay me to do a portrait. But I also love doing horses, which I think are the hardest animals to get right. Horses and lions. The easiest are fish, but to be honest I find them a little boring.

I AM A BUILDER

I'm Viggo Augur. Builders like me are never famous, although Rome has many famous buildings and I helped to build a lot of them.

This year I'm working on a handsome new aqueduct which the Emperor himself has ordered to bring more water into the city. There are already several of these in Rome and together they stretch for hundreds of miles. A few are underground tunnels, large enough for a big man like me to walk through, but this new one is more like a really long bridge.

When the aqueduct is finished it will have nearly a hundred tall arches and a channel running along the top of it to carry fresh water down from the hills.

Sometimes we build with bricks and wood and at other times with huge blocks of carved stone. Today we're using *opus caementicium*, a type of concrete that we mix with ash from a volcano to make it durable

and tremendously strong. It's such a smart Roman invention that I like to think my buildings will still be standing in a thousand years or more.

Many of the other men working here are slaves; quite a few of them are prisoners captured in the Emperor's recent wars. But Rome likes to have Romans in charge, and that's my job. I tell the slaves what to do, and then I make sure they are doing it right. It's an important job. It's like I tell my children: there aren't many things a city needs more than water and—with a million citizens—Rome needs more of it than ever!

Without bath houses, Romans can't wash. Without latrines, they can't go to the bathroom. Everything needs water—cooking, cleaning, making pots out of clay, even mixing volcanic ash into concrete! Other cities might wait for rain, but the greatest city on Earth can't wait. Somehow there is never enough water to go round.

23

I AM A LEGIONARY

An empire as big as this one depends on soldiers like me, Secundus Nigilius.

I'm a foot solder, or legionary, and as you can see, I'm well-armed. I have a shield made of wood and leather, two javelins or spears, a dagger, and a short sword of strong steel. The officers in charge of us say this is the best army in the world, and I believe them. We train hard and we have the best weapons. We also have the finest armor, although it's heavy and can be uncomfortable under the hot sun or when we're marching through a storm.

Years ago, the legionaries all came from Rome, but as the empire grew larger the army grew with it. Now the army has more than 400,000 men, and new recruits come from all over the empire.

Me? I'm from northern Africa yet I fight alongside men from Gaul (France), Britannia (Britain) and all the other countries the Emperor's army has conquered.

When we're not fighting, we're marching. That's tough too because we have to carry all our equipment and supplies on our backs. Often we march nearly 30 miles a day, each man carrying not just his weapons but

also a heavy goatskin full of drinking water mixed with vinegar, and a spade and wood to build fortifications. We also carry enough food for 14 days (and something to cook it in) because every legionary loves his food.

So you can see it's a hard life, but a good one too. I joined the army aged 20 and when I leave aged 45, I'll be given some land to call my own. That's how it works: I serve the emperor, then the emperor rewards me. My plan is to build a house, plant grape vines and olive trees on my land, and then see if I can find myself a wife.

I AM A MERCHANT

Merchants and ship owners like me make a living buying and selling goods. I am Vesuvia Blanda and you might have seen my ship down in the harbor, the *Salacia*. It's named after the goddess of saltwater.

In Roman society there are certain jobs that women are not allowed to do, and many do no more than get married and have children. Girls marry early here (as young as 12) but I knew this was not for me, and so I have never done it. Instead I run my own business buying wheat from Egypt and sailing it back across the Mediterranean so it can be sold at a profit.

There are many merchants who are women like me, but of course even more who are men. As for ship owners, I know of only one other who is a woman: she is a tall Egyptian called Sarapias. However, most trade of this sort is done by men. The captain of the *Salacia* is a man, his crew are all men, and the slaves who load and unload my wheat for me—they are men too.

The journey back from Egypt takes a week or more. Wooden ships are often wrecked in storms and sailors often become sick, but so far we've been lucky. Romans eat a lot of bread and pancakes, and to make these you need wheat. My customers pay extra for the best, and they know my Egyptian wheat is top quality. This means the day the *Salacia* arrives at the port of Ostia near Rome, I can get the highest price, which is what I like.

And here's a tip for you: a successful merchant never sends an empty ship to sea. Before the *Salacia* goes back to Egypt my slaves will load it up with wood and metal household items, as well as a box or two of precious jewels. Rich Egyptians pay good prices for Roman craftsmanship, you know, and where there's money to be made you'll always find a merchant.

I AM AN ARMY OFFICER

The Roman Empire would not exist without its army, and it can't survive without us. We fight the Emperor's enemies, we impose order, and we enforce the law. My name is Marcus Salonius Remus, and I am proud to be an officer.

My rank is a high one and well-respected. My scarlet cloak shows that I am a Legatus Legionis, meaning I command a legion of 5,000 soldiers. These are all strong and courageous men, they are fit and they fight like giants. Many times I have seen how they strike fear into our enemies, and at least twice I have watched the other side turn and run away rather than face its own destruction.

This legion has fought its way through many lands while I have been in command, from Mesopotamia in the east to Hispania in the west. I am pleased to say we have never been defeated in all that time, although many brave men have died horribly or been badly wounded.

Roman soldiers train hard and are always ready for battle, but there are many other tasks to be done when there is no fighting. My men have built fortifications in the lands we conquered, and even hospitals. They've laid out miles of fine, straight roads connecting these to Rome, and constructed sturdy stone bridges wherever a road crosses a river. So, trust me when I say a good legionary is as skilled as any engineer. It is the truth.

The roads and bridges are used by ordinary Romans all the time, but that isn't the main reason we build them. A straight road is the quickest route between two places. Using ours, we can out-march and out-manoeuvre Rome's enemies. By being first to the battlefield, we can be armed and ready before the other side has even woken up!

I AM A PHYSICIAN

I'm Benignus Volo and I am the man rich Romans turn to when they get sick.

The people of Rome know that all the best doctors in the city are Greeks, and that I come from a Greek family. They know I learned many of my skills at the valetudinarium in Novae, a large and important army hospital. They also know that Benignus means "kind" in Latin, although my sharp tools scare them and they hear stories about surgical operations going badly wrong.

Unfortunately no one treats the poor, who have no money for doctors. There are no public hospitals for them so mostly they just pray to the gods and hope they will get well again. Sometimes this seems to work, but not often. Usually they get sicker and then die. It is sad that life is so cruel to them, but not even the best doctor will work without payment.

Many of my cures sound simple enough. I always recommend cold cucumber to cure a hot fever, and hot pepper to cure a cold, but others are more mysterious.

Sometimes I recommend egg yolks, or boiled liver for painful eyes, and rhubarb for stomach pains. I once used dirty wool from a sheep to treat a woman with diseased skin, and I know one doctor who says that eating mice whole is good for toothache. Other good medicines can be made from herbs and tree bark, which I often soak first in wine.

Many of these herbs taste bitter but it is always much worse when I have to cut someone with my knives. Five or six slaves are needed to hold the frightened patient down because even the best surgeon with the finest tools takes a long time to saw through solid bone. I'm afraid that only the strongest patient will survive the pain, and a man's blood can become poisonous, assuming there is any blood left...

I AM A GOVERNOR

When the Roman army defeats its enemies in battle, the conquered country becomes a province of the Empire. Soon afterwards, the Emperor appoints a governor to rule his new province, and for Germania he chose me—Flavius Marius Tenebris.

No one is more important than the Emperor, but I am the most senior official in Germania —an area which you now call Germany—and by far its most powerful man. When the empire needs more money, I raise it in taxes that the Germanians have to pay. I command a legion of 5,000 well-trained and heavily armed soldiers who keep order across the province. I also sit in judgement over the population and have the power to have the worst criminals put to death.

This does not make me a popular man, but that is not something that worries me. I am certain that the tribes of Germania will welcome us eventually. They will see that the Roman way is the right way, for them as well as for the Empire. Our new buildings are superior to the ones they make of wet mud and with thatched roofs. Their towns will be safer, cleaner, and more beautiful under our rule. The excellent new roads the army is building will make it easier for ordinary people to travel and help merchants to carry out their business.

I know being part of the Roman Empire will improve life in this province because I grew up in a province myself. As a young boy, I saw how much richer Numidia became when the Romans conquered us. They renamed it Africa Nova and built fine new towns where we had only empty deserts. They built roads to the coast, and large harbors so that Numidians could trade with the rest of the empire. Numidians were even allowed to become Romans citizens themselves, and a few—like me— worked hard to become powerful and extremely rich.

I AM A SCRIBE

Most Romans can't read and write, so a scribe can make a good living doing it for them. I am Cordia Verbis and I work as a scribe.

It is an unusual job for a woman, as most scribes in Rome are men. I was lucky that my father, a famous poet, taught me to read and write as a child. He thought they were important skills to have—and I agree! Not everyone feels the same, though. Often in Roman society, even very rich people cannot read and some can only write their names.

When I was growing up I thought I would become a teacher and pass on my skills to others, but nobody wants a woman teacher in Rome or anywhere else I know. Luckily, there are many other things a woman can do if she can read and write. For example, I can read my father's poetry (which I love) but I can also read the letters and documents that people bring to my home.

They pay me to do this for them, and then they pay again if they need to send an answer. Merchants also pay me to write the legal contracts they need for business, but sometimes they are suspicious. Most are not used to discussing their work with a woman. They think I won't understand what they are saying, or that I will sell their secrets to a rival!

I mix my own ink, using soot and glue, and a goose feather cut to a sharp point makes a fine pen for writing on papyrus, a kind of paper made from flattened plants called reeds. I can also make red ink by grinding a stone called cinnabar into powder, but I don't do this very often. The stone is expensive and the grinding takes so long. It also makes me feel sick, and I think the stone might be poisonous.

I AM A BAKER

Romans all eat bread so a baker's job is a busy one, no matter where he lives.
I'm Spurius Noster, by the way, and I've been baking for more than 20 years.

I worked with my father when I first started, but he died a long time ago. Housewives used to mix their own dough at home and my father taught me how to bake it for them in our oven. It doesn't work like that anymore though. These days, I only bake my own bread at the back of my shop and customers buy as much of it as they need or can afford.

It's not a job that just anyone can do. Because bread is such an important part of our diet, there are rules about how it is made and who is allowed to make it. Bakers like me have to belong to the Collegium Pistorum, an organization which helps to ensure that all the bread and pastries sold in Rome are of the right quality.

My best bread is the white bread, which I bake for my richest customers using the finest wheat from Egypt. Most of these loaves are round and flat, but sometimes I bake different shapes for special occasions. I like doing this and enjoy making different types of bread for eating with oysters (we Romans love shellfish!) and other breads mixed with milk, eggs, or cheese.

These are very expensive and not all my customers are rich. I bake brown bread for the hungry ones who can't afford to buy the best. It's made using cheaper grains such as oats and rye, or even acorns at the right time of year. It's very filling (and it sells very well) but it can be hard and dry, so I tell my customers to dip it in olive oil before they take a bite.

I AM A BANKER

Trade is an important part of life in the Roman Empire, so there is always plenty of business for a banker like me, Lucretius Tappo.

I look after money for some customers and lend money to others when they need it. Everyone has to pay back a bit more than he borrows, so that's my profit. Most of these people are merchants but I'll lend to anyone as long as he looks like he will pay me back. Each loan is made using gold and silver coins (we don't have paper money) and if anyone complains about the weight, I just tell him to buy more slaves to carry it!

I also work as a moneychanger, which means I sell Roman coins to foreigners who pay using money from their own countries. I can't spend this in Rome so I look for a merchant who is traveling overseas in search of goods to bring back and sell. He'll need my foreign money to pay for this and he'll give me Roman coins in exchange. Every time I do it, I make another profit.

I keep some money in a secret locked chest at my house, but most of it is in a room beneath the local temple. People have always used temples as safe places to store money and other treasures because we trust the priests not to steal. Also, Romans are religious and with so many worshippers at the temple every day (and soldiers patrolling outside) it would be difficult for a thief to break in without being seen.

I know the Emperor thinks this, too. How do I know? Because in Rome the place where all the gold and silver coins are made is another temple, one called Juno Moneta. It's where your English word "money" comes from, and it's always been one of my favorites.

39

I AM A WEALTHY LADY

My name is Tullia Domitilla and I am one of the richest women in all of Rome.

Many years ago, my great-great-grandfather was emperor. So you can tell our family has been rich for a long time. Like all other Roman women, I cannot vote or stand for election, but my wealth gives me more power than most women have in our society. Many of Rome's most important politicians are my friends, for example, and several have asked for my advice or followed my suggestions.

These men know that I am not just rich but also a good businesswoman. I don't like to be idle, and I own many properties in Rome as well as vast estates in the countryside. My slaves mostly grow grapes to make wine and olives for the oil that Romans burn in their lamps. Both of these crops fetch high prices and I use the profits to buy more land and more buildings in and around the city.

Most of these buildings are tall blocks of aparments called *insulae*. I rent these out to ordinary families, people who cannot afford a house like mine. Each family has just two rooms to live in but my own home is much larger and naturally very luxurious.

My beautiful house has central heating. Each winter, three slaves are kept busy minding the fires that drive hot smoke under the floor to warm the rooms. These rooms contain elegant furniture and sculptures, and outside there is a spacious courtyard with a covered veranda where I can sit with friends and relax.

I have my own private bath too, which is a very unusual feature for a house. Even so, I still visit the public bath house at least once a week. Most Romans do this as it is an excellent place to meet people and to do business. It is also the best way to hear the political news of the day, which I always find interesting, and to learn what else is happening throughout the empire.

I AM A GLADIATOR

More than 50,000 spectators fill the Colosseum whenever the emperor comes here to see gladiators like me put on our armor and fight to the death. Romans really love their public entertainments.

Our shows are free and include many types of gladiators. Some fight with swords or spears or giant forks called tridents. Others try to trap their opponents using ropes or nets. A few ride horses, but most do not. Usually the gladiators fight man against man, but not me. I am Maximus the Bestiarius and I fight wild animals.

I am very well paid for this and the thousands who come to watch me call me a hero. However, it is hard work even for a strong man like me, and many of the bravest young gladiators have been killed doing what I do. Some of them were my friends.

It probably seems a strange thing to you, wanting to see a man die like this, but it has always been the Roman way. The people enjoy watching chariot races too, and also dancing girls, but nothing matches the

noise and excitement of gladiators fighting. The cheer of the crowd can be louder than thunder. Sometimes it seems to me as if the whole city is packed into the arena. Men as well as women, the rich as well as the poor. Everyone watching closely, and waiting for the blood to flow.

The animals I fight are the most exotic and dangerous ones in the world. I've fought lions from Africa, bears from Asia, panthers, crocodiles, and even a horned rhinoceros, which I killed with a single stab from a spear. My friend Carpophorus once killed twenty beasts in a single battle. I watched him do this and admire him greatly for it, but it's a record I would really love to beat.

I AM A PRIESTESS

My name is Flavia Leptis and all year you will find me at the great Temple of Diana.

My family came across the sea from North Africa many years ago. Our father made his fortune working near a city called Capua in southern Italy. He employed hundreds of slaves making bricks, tiles, and clay pots. When my father died, I sold the factory and moved to the city. Most of the money was spent building a new temple to the goddess Diana with a large public fountain in the courtyard outside.

For as long as anyone can remember, most of the important jobs in the Roman Empire have been given to men. It is the same in Capua. Women from the most powerful families are not allowed to become politicians or even to vote in elections. However, religion plays a large part in Roman lives so priestesses like me can become important members of society.

In my case it helps that Diana is one of the highest-ranking of the gods. We Romans worship dozens of different gods and goddesses, but they are not all equal. Diana's status makes me more important than many other priests and priestesses. Also my knowledge of bricks and tiles ensured that my temple was larger and more impressive than any others in Capua.

As a priestess I perform religious rituals inside the temple. We have many festivals throughout the year where every ritual must be carefully performed. Romans believe that the success of our city and of the empire depends on the goodwill of many different gods. We would lose their support if we ignore the rituals or if priests perform them badly. If that happens we would perish.

WOULD YOU LIKE TO BE A ROMAN?

You've met a powerful emperor and a powerless slave boy, a rich lady with time to sit back and relax, and a legionary who has to march for miles, carrying a heavy pack. Now you've got to know a few of them, would *you* like to try your luck at living life as a Roman?

What you might have noticed from this book is that there were lots of differences between the lives of different Romans. Whether a person was rich or poor, and whether they had powerful connections or not, could have a huge impact on their quality of life. But even powerful people like the Emperor didn't always have a great life—they were often busy looking over their shoulder in case someone wanted to get rid of them!

Rome depended on a vast number of slaves to do work for the more powerful citizens. If you were a slave, whether you had a miserable life or a good one would have hinged on what sort of master you had. Either way, you had no power to choose what you did with your life. If you were lucky, one day you would be granted your freedom.

So, whether you would opt to be a wealthy merchant or a hardworking scribe, one thing is certain: if you could go back in time and try out being a Roman for yourself, you wouldn't have the same access to medicine as you have today, so you'd better hope you didn't get sick. And while you could be entertained by musicians and dancers, shocked by the ferocious gladiator fights, or gaze at beautiful mosaic pictures, you would be a few thousand years too early to grab a snack from the fridge, put your feet up in front of the television, and chat to your friends on your phone!

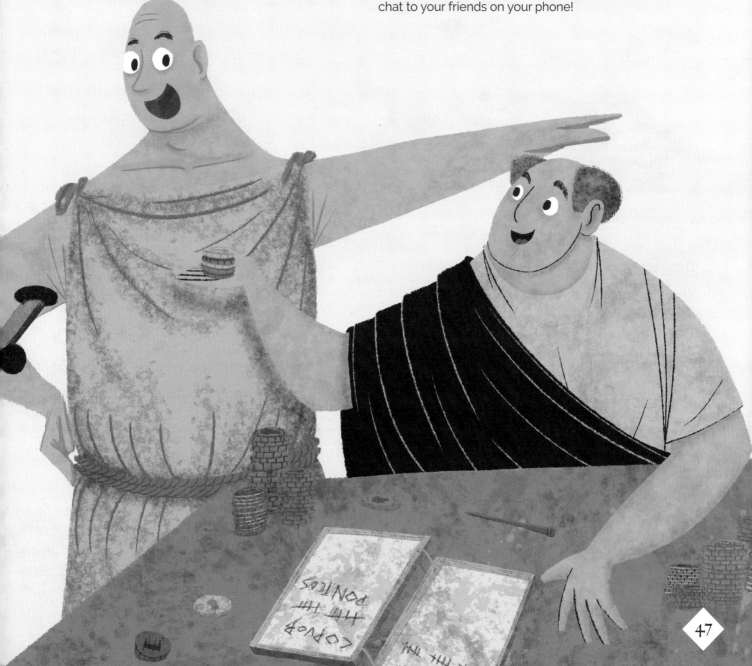

Hadrian's Wall

BRITANNIA
(England and Wales)

Atlantic Ocean

GAUL
(France and parts of
surrounding countries)

DALMATIA
(Balkan countries)

Rome ○

ITALIA
(Italy)

Pompeii ●
Mt. Vesuvius

HISPANIA
(Spain and Portugal)

ACHAEA
(part of Greece)

Tyrrhenian Sea

SICILIA

Mediterranean Sea

AFRICA
(Tunisia)

NUMIDIA
(Algeria)

TRIPOLITANIA
(Libya)

Note: There were not the same
borders between countries in Roman times as
there are today. The modern country names in
brackets give a rough guide only.

48

THE ROMAN EMPIRE

At the peak of its power, the Roman Empire stretched far beyond the city of Rome, spreading its influence across many lands that today make up Europe, the Middle East, and northern Africa.

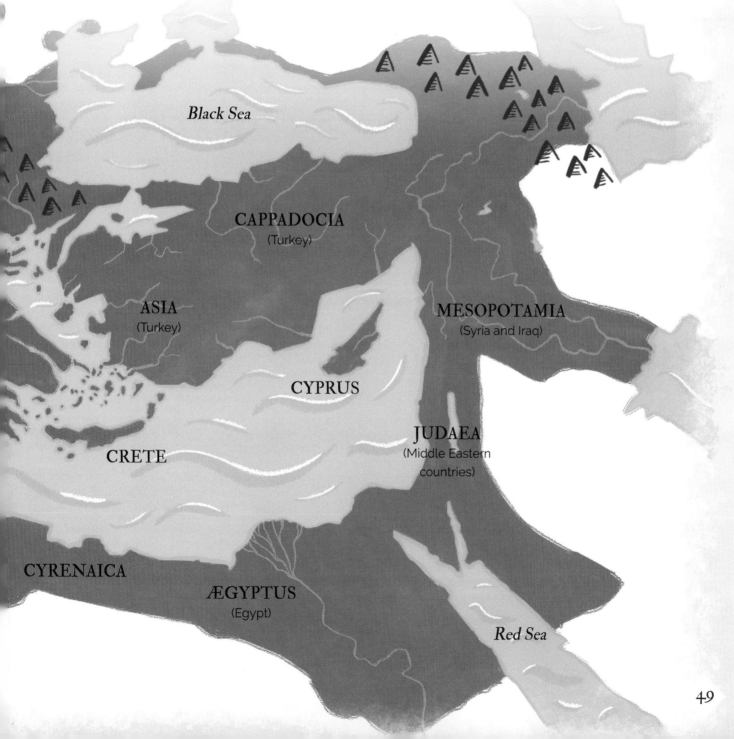

Black Sea

CAPPADOCIA
(Turkey)

ASIA
(Turkey)

MESOPOTAMIA
(Syria and Iraq)

CYPRUS

JUDAEA
(Middle Eastern
countries)

CRETE

CYRENAICA

ÆGYPTUS
(Egypt)

Red Sea

TIMELINE

Read about the key points in Roman history, from the founding of Rome to the expansion of the empire until its fall.

753 BCE
The city of Rome is founded. For more than 200 years it is ruled by kings.

509 BCE
Rome becomes a republic when the last king is replaced by elected officials called senators.

312 BCE
The first aqueduct is completed to supply a growing population with fresh water.

43 CE
The Romans launch their invasion of Britain.

27 BCE
The beginning of the Roman Empire. Its first emperor is Caesar Augustus.

30 BCE
The Romans invade Egypt which becomes an important source of food.

50 CE
Londinium is founded as an important Roman trading port, close to where the Tower of London stands today.

61 CE
Boudica, a Celtic rebel leader, attacks Londinium and burns much of it to the ground.

64 CE
Much of Rome is destroyed in another disastrous fire. Hundreds of buildings are damaged, including Emperor Nero's palace.

380 CE
Emperor Theodosius makes Christianity the official religion of the Roman Empire.

306 CE
Constantine is named as emperor while at York in England. He later abandons pagan worship and becomes a Christian.

238 CE
13-year-old Emperor Gordian III becomes Rome's youngest ever ruler but he dies less than six years later.

401 CE
The Romans begin leaving Britain.

410 CE
Visigoth tribes attack the city of Rome. It is the first time in 800 years that the capital has fallen to an enemy.

476 CE
Rome's last emperor, Romulus Augustulus, is defeated by a German army. This marks the end of the empire and the beginning of the Dark Ages.

218 BCE
An African general called Hannibal attacks the republic after his army crosses the Alps on elephants.

146 BCE
The Romans invade Greece and become enthusiastic admirers of Greek art and architecture.

73 BCE
Spartacus the Gladiator leads a rebellion of slaves against their owners.

45 BCE
Julius Caesar declares he is Rome's new ruler but is murdered the following year by friends who think he has become too powerful.

50 BCE
Romans introduce their first soild gold coin, called the aureus.

59 BCE
The first Roman newspapers are written on metal or stone. These are placed on outside walls for educated Romans to read.

79 CE
Mount Vesuvius erupts, covering the city of Pompeii in several feet of volcanic ash and stone. At least 16,000 men, women, and children are killed.

80 CE
The Colosseum is built, one of the largest buildings in the world. It can seat 50,000 spectators who watch gladiators fighting and other public entertainments.

100 CE
More than 8,000 miles of new Roman roads make it easier than ever to move troops and goods around Britain.

125 CE
The Pantheon in Rome is completed, a circular temple with the largest domed roof in the world.

121 CE
Roman legionaries build Hadrian's Wall, an important line of fortifications across northern Britain.

117 CE
The empire is at its largest under Emperor Trajan. It covers approximately two million square miles of Europe, Asia, and Africa.

FAMOUS PEOPLE IN ROMAN TIMES

Discover some of the most famous people that lived and worked in Roman times.

SPARTACUS (111–71 BCE)

Spartacus was a soldier who was enslaved and trained to be a gladiator. He escaped and led a rebellion with an army of other escaped slaves, before being defeated in battle.

JULIUS CAESAR (100–44 BCE)

Caesar was a renowned general and politician, who conquered the Gauls. On his return to Rome, he seized control, making himself a dictator and was later assassinated (killed).

MARK ANTONY (82–30 BCE)

This politician and general was a great supporter of Julius Caesar. When Caesar died, Antony battled for power with Caesar's adopted son and heir, Octavian. He later fled to Egypt as Octavian's armies invaded Alexandria, and died in queen Cleopatra's arms.

CLEOPATRA (69–30 BCE)

The last true pharaoh of Egypt, Cleopatra was known for her intelligence. She had romantic and political relationships with Julius Caesar and Mark Antony. She chose to die, by venomous snakebite, rather than be captured when threatened by Octavian's armies.

AUGUSTUS (63 BCE–14 CE)

The first emperor of Rome, he previously went by the name Octavian. After defeating Antony and Cleopatra, he went on to rule the empire for 40 years. The month of August is named after him.

OVID (43 BCE–17 CE)

A famous Roman poet whose works are still read today.

HORTENSIA (1st century BCE)

The first woman to make a speech in the Roman Forum. In 42 BCE, she successfully argued against taxing the property of the wealthiest Roman women to pay for a civil war.

NERO (37–68 CE)

Emperor Nero was known as the madman of Rome. During his rule, two thirds of Rome burned down while he sat in his palace doing nothing to stop it. Some think he even started the fire.

HADRIAN (76–138 CE)

Emperor Hadrian rebuilt the Pantheon in Rome, but is most known for building "Hadrian's Wall," a 73-mile-long fortification that marked the northern limit of the Roman empire in Britain.

HYPATIA (370–415 CE)

Famous inventor and astronomer, she taught mathematics and philosophy in the city of Alexandria, in Egypt.

ROMAN INVENTIONS

We owe a lot to the technology and practices developed by Ancient Romans. Here are just a few that have made their mark on the modern world.

CENTRAL HEATING

Wealthy Romans were able to keep their homes warm in winter with the invention of an underfloor heating system, called a hypocaust. The floors were supported on columns of tiles, and a furnace circulated hot air underneath. Very handy if you're building a house in a cold, northern part of the Empire!

AQUEDUCTS

Aqueduct means "water way" in Latin. An aqueduct is an ancient water transport system, bringing water from lakes and streams into the cities. Having a constant supply of fresh water meant that waste could be washed away into drains and sewers, keeping cities and their people clean.

CONCRETE

Roman concrete was so strong that many of their buildings, such as the Colosseum, Pantheon, and the Roman Forum, are still standing thousands of years later. It was made out of chunks of rock, brick, and other rubble, mixed with a cement of volcanic ash and water.

ARCHES

Arches are everywhere in Roman engineering. Romans discovered how effective arches could be and worked out ways to make them better and stronger. Many Roman bridges, aqueducts, and buildings made use of arches, and some still survive today.

POSTAL SERVICE

Since the Roman Empire was so large, people needed a reliable way of staying in touch with each other. Emperor Augustus created the *cursus publicus* (the public way), where a delivery man would carry messages and official documents to their destination.

GODS & GODDESSES

Romans believed in many different gods and goddesses, and felt every success was a result of keeping the gods happy. They worshipped 12 main gods and goddesses.

JUPITER

King of the gods, Jupiter was the god of the sky and thunder. He wielded a lightning bolt as his weapon.

Greek name: Zeus
Sacred animal: Eagle

JUNO

Goddess of fertility, protector of women, and the patron goddess of Rome. Juno was also the wife of Jupiter and mother of Mars and Vulcan.

Greek name: Hera
Sacred animal: Peacock

MARS

God of war, son of Jupiter and Juno, and the father of twin brothers Romulus and Remus, who founded Rome. Mars was also the guardian of soldiers and farmers.

Greek name: Ares
Sacred animals: Wolf, woodpecker, bear

VENUS

Goddess of love, beauty, and prosperity. Venus was the mother of Cupid, the god of love and desire.

Greek name: Aphrodite
Sacred animal: Dove

APOLLO

Apollo was sometimes known to the Romans as Phoebus. He was the god of music, poetry, archery, healing and the Sun.

Greek name: Apollo
Sacred animals: Hawk, crow, snake, swan, wolf, dolphin

DIANA

Goddess of hunting, wild animals, and the Moon. Diana was often shown holding a bow and quiver of arrows.

Greek name: Artemis
Sacred animals: Deer, hunting dogs

MERCURY

God of travelers, communication, and trade, the messenger of the gods is often shown with winged sandals on his feet.

Greek name: Hermes
Sacred animals: Tortoise, ram, rooster

CERES

Goddess of the seasons, agriculture, and harvest. Ceres was thought to have discovered how to plant crops and farm the land.

Greek name: Demeter
Sacred animal: Pig

VESTA

Goddess of the hearth and home, Vesta is one of the oldest gods. She was the patron goddess of bakers, and revered in every Roman's home.

Greek name: Hestia
Sacred animal: Donkey

VULCAN

God of fire, blacksmiths, and volcanoes. Vulcan manufactured armor and weapons for gods and heroes, including Jupiter's lightning bolts.

Greek name: Hephaestus
Sacred animals: Dog, crane

MINERVA

Goddess of wisdom, strategy, medicine, and a sponsor of art and crafts. Minerva was the daughter of Jupiter. The legend goes that she sprang from her father's head fully armed.

Greek name: Athena
Sacred animal: Owl

NEPTUNE

God of freshwater and the sea. This brother of Jupiter was shown driving a seahorse-drawn chariot. Because of this, Neptune was a patron of horse-racing.

Greek name: Poseidon
Sacred animals: Dolphin, horse

LEARN LATIN

Romans spoke Latin, a language that is now only used to give scientific names to things, and in Rome's Vatican City during religious ceremonies.

Romans originally wrote in capital letters only, with dots to show spaces between each word. This was because they most commonly wrote on wax tablets that didn't have a lot of space. Lower case letters and punctuation weren't used until much later on. They used 23 letters instead of the 26 in the modern Roman alphabet. The letters J, U, and W didn't make it into the alphabet until medieval times.

Many modern languages developed from Latin, such as French, Spanish, Portuguese, Italian, and Romanian. These are known as the Romance languages. Knowing a bit of Latin can make it easier to learn Romance languages, as they are similar.

HELLO	SALVE
GOODBYE	VALE
WHAT'S YOUR NAME?	QUOD EST TIBI NOMEN?
MY NAME IS . . .	MIHI NOMEN EST . . .
HOW ARE YOU?	QUID AGIS?
I'M FINE	BENE SUM
WHAT TIME IS IT?	QUID TEMPORUM EST?
LEFT	SINISTER
RIGHT	DEXTER
FIRST	PRIMUS
SECOND	SECUNDUS
THIRD	TERTIUS

CAVE•CANEM:
"BEWARE THE DOG"

Archaeologists at the ruined city of Pompeii discovered an incredible mosaic on the floor in the entrance to a house. It depicted a dog on a leash with a written warning for people to enter at their own risk.

ROMAN NUMERALS

People used Roman numerals until well after the decline of the Roman Empire, but they were gradually replaced by the Arabic numerals that most of the world use today.

1	I	80	LXXX
2	II	90	XC
3	III	100	C
4	IV		
5	V	200	CC
6	VI	300	CCC
7	VII	400	CD
8	VIII	500	D
9	IX	600	DC
10	X	700	DCC
		800	DCCC
20	XX	900	CM
30	XXX		
40	XL	1000	M
50	L	2000	MM
60	LX	3000	MMM
70	LXX		

HOW TO COUNT LIKE A ROMAN

When a symbol appears after a larger or equal symbol, it is added.

VI = V + I

If the symbol appears before a larger symbol, it is subtracted.

IV = V - I

The same symbol cannot be used more than three times in a row.

THE ROMAN ARMY

There might have been around half a million soldiers in the Roman army at any one time. These well-trained fighting machines were one of the reasons the Roman Empire became so powerful.

The helmet was called a *galea*. Soldiers sometimes added a crest of horse hair to the top of it, like this one.

Known as a *pilum*, the spear was made out of wood with an iron spike tip.

The army was divided into large groups of about 5,000 men, called legions. These were divided into smaller groups called centuries. The man in charge was known as a centurion.

All soldiers in the Roman army had to be in shape to march all day carrying their equipment, and have enough energy to fight, and make camp. As well as fighting, soldiers built roads, bridges, fortifications, and aqueducts.

Soldiers had to wear heavy armor made of overlapping iron plates. They wore a tunic underneath to stop the metal from chafing.

A soldier's curved, rectangular shield was called a *scutum*. Soldiers would protect themselves from arrows by lifting it above their head, like a tortoise shell.

ROMAN FOOD

A lot of the food Romans ate isn't that different from a modern Mediterranean diet, but you might not enjoy some of their more exotic dishes!

Romans ate three meals a day. Breakfast was called *ientaculum*, lunch was known as *prandium*, and dinner, called *cena*, was the largest meal of the day. Poor Romans mostly ate a savory oatmeal-like stew called pottage, which was made of wheat, millet, and corn with added vegetables.

Rich Romans ate a much wider range of food. Their *cena* included many courses and often lasted hours. Some of the dishes included olives, oysters, sea urchins, peacock, snails, and flamingo tongues. A popular delicacy was baked dormice dipped in honey—delicious!

BAKE BREAD LIKE A ROMAN

Ingredients

3 cups + 2 tbsps (500g) spelt flour
1 1/2 cups (350ml) water
1 1/2 tbsp olive oil
salt

I. Preheat your oven to 350 °F (180 °C).

II. In a large bowl add the spelt flour and a pinch of salt and mix it together with clean hands.

II. Pour the olive oil into the bowl.

III. Gradually add the water and keep mixing with your hands until the dough is not too sticky or floury.

IV. Knead the dough into a circular shape and place it on a lightly floured baking tray.

V. Now to make your mark: use a knife to slice the top of the dough into eight sections.

VI. Put your loaf in the oven for 45 minutes.

GLOSSARY

cena: the Roman word for dinner.

century (plural centuries): a sub-group of a legion, within the Roman army.

centurion: the soldier in charge of a century.

cinnabar: a type of stone used to make red ink, used by scribes.

Collegium Pistorum: an organization for bakers, which helped to ensure that all the bread and pastries sold in Rome were of the right quality.

cursus publicus: Latin for "the public way." This service was created by Emperor Augustus, where a delivery man would carry messages and official documents to their destination.

galea: the helmet worn by soldiers in the Roman army.

hypocaust: an underfloor heating system invented by the Romans.

ientaculum: the Roman word for breakfast.

insulae: tall blocks of apartments, usually owned by rich Romans and rented out to people who could not afford houses.

Juno Moneta: the temple in Rome where all the gold and silver coins are made. The English word "money" comes from "Moneta."

Legatus Legionis: the officer who commands a legion within the Roman army.

legions: the divisions within the Roman army. Each legion was a group of about 5,000 foot soldiers, called legionaries.

liberta: a freed slave.

Numidians: the people of Numidia. The Romans renamed Numidia "Africa Nova" when they conquered it.

opus caementicium: a type of concrete mixed with volcanic ash to make it durable and extremely strong, used by the Romans for building structures such as aqueducts.

papyrus: a kind of paper made from reeds.

patricians: the wealthiest members of society.

pilum: a spear made out of wood with an iron spike tip, used by the soldiers in the Roman army.

plebians: the ordinary people of the Roman society ruled by patricians.

prandium: the Roman word for lunch.

scabellum: a rhythmic wooden foot clapper, a type of Roman musical instrument.

scutum: a curved, rectangular shield carried by the soldiers in the Roman army.

Senate: a major governing and advisory body to the kings and emperors of the Roman empire, typically made up of important and wealthy men from powerful Roman families.

senator: a member of the Senate.

stylus: a sharp tool used by the Romans to write on wax tablets.

tablet: a flat piece of wood or bone covered in wax used for writing. These "tablets" were notably used in Roman schools instead of papyrus, because they were cheaper to make.

tesserae: tiny cubes of cut rock, stone, or glass used to make a mosaic.

tibia: a type of Roman musical instrument made from two pipes joined together, side by side.

valetudinarium: a hospital for the sick and wounded. The Romans only set up valetudinarium as army hospitals in times of war, when their armies marched beyond the boundaries of their empire. There were no public hospitals in the empire for the ordinary people.

Visigoths: an early Germanic people (part of the Goths) who raided Roman territories and established great kingdoms in Gaul (France) and Hispania (Spain and Portugal).

FIND OUT MORE

Visit these museums, websites, and historic sites to discover more about the Romans.

MUSEUMS

BRITISH MUSEUM
London, England

MUSEUM OF LONDON
London, England

METROPOLITAN MUSEUM OF ART
New York

WALTERS ART MUSEUM
Baltimore

FIELD MUSEUM
Chicago

ROMAN SITES IN THE UK

HADRIAN'S WALL
Northern England

ROMAN BATHS
Bath

ANTONINE WALL
Scotland

CHEDWORTH ROMAN VILLA
Cheltenham, Gloucestershire

FISHBOURNE ROMAN PALACE
Chichester, West Sussex

WHEN IN ROME

COLOSSEUM
An ancient Roman gladiatorial arena.

PANTHEON
The most well-preserved Roman structure that was a temple to all the gods.

ROMAN FORUM
Ruins of the temples, palaces, and stores that formed the hub of the Roman empire.

BATHS OF CARACALLA
Ruins of a once massive spa, with saunas, baths, and an Olympic sized swimming pool.

APPIAN WAY
One of the earliest and most important of Roman roads that you can still walk on today.

WEBSITES

BRITISH MUSEUM
www.britishmuseum.org/learn/schools/ages-7-11/ancient-rome

NATIONAL GEOGRAPHIC KIDS
www.natgeokids.com/uk/discover/history/romans

ENCYCLOPEDIA BRITANNICA
www.kids.britannica.com/kids/article/ancient-Rome/353728

INDEX